3

6

BUGS BUNNY

body

ears

mouth

nose, tongue

ELMER FUDD

body

mouth, gun, shoes

tongue

hunting outfit

hat panel

gun barrel

DAFFY DUCK

beak, feet, legs

mouth

tongue

SPEEDY GONZALES

body

scarf

mouth

tongue

hat

ear

WILE E. COYOTE

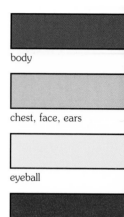

body

chest, face, ears

eyeball

eyemask

ROAD RUNNER

body

head comb, wings

mouth

tongue

beak

legs

SYLVESTER JR.

nose

mouth

tongue

PORKY PIG
PETUNIA PIG

bodies

mouths

tongues

Petunia's shirt

flower stem, leaves

Porky's jacket, cap

Porky's tie,
Petunia's skirt, flower

13

YOSEMITE SAM

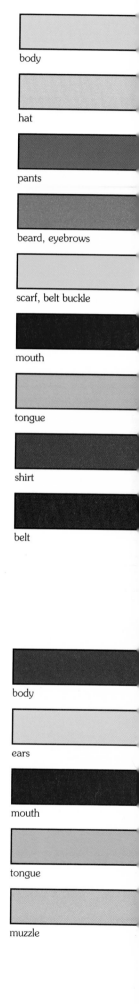

body

hat

pants

beard, eyebrows

scarf, belt buckle

mouth

tongue

shirt

belt

TASMANIAN DEVIL

body

ears

mouth

tongue

muzzle

14

SHE-DEVIL

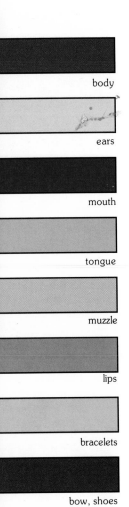

body

ears

mouth

tongue

muzzle

lips

bracelets

bow, shoes

MARVIN THE MARTIAN

helmet, skirt

helmet brush

brush base

shirt, legs, shoes

15

PEPE LE PEW
PENELOPE

mouths

tongues

FOGHORN LEGHORN
HENERY HAWK

FOGHORN

feet, beak

mouth

tongue

tail, head

head comb, beard comb

HENERY

body

beak, feet

16

SYLVESTER

nose

mouth

tongue

TWEETY

body

eyes

mouth

tongue

beak, feet

17

Not intended for resale.

THE MARTIAN UNIVERSITY

MARVIN

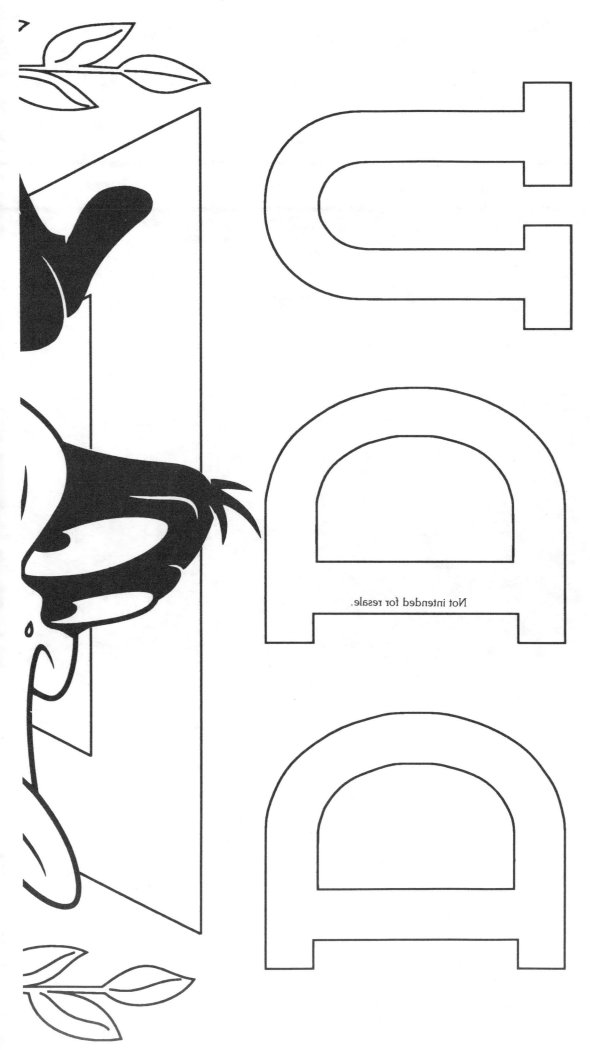

DAFFY DUCK UNIVERSITY

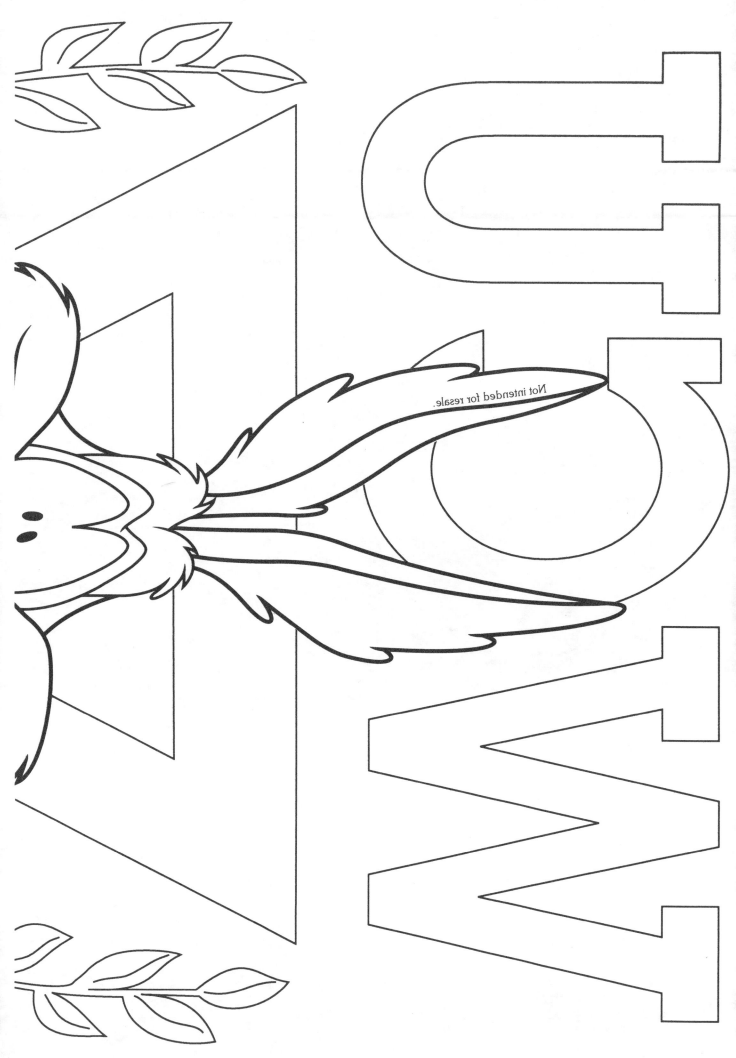

Not intended for resale.

24

WILE E. COYOTE UNIVERSITY

TM & © 1995 Warner Bros.

25

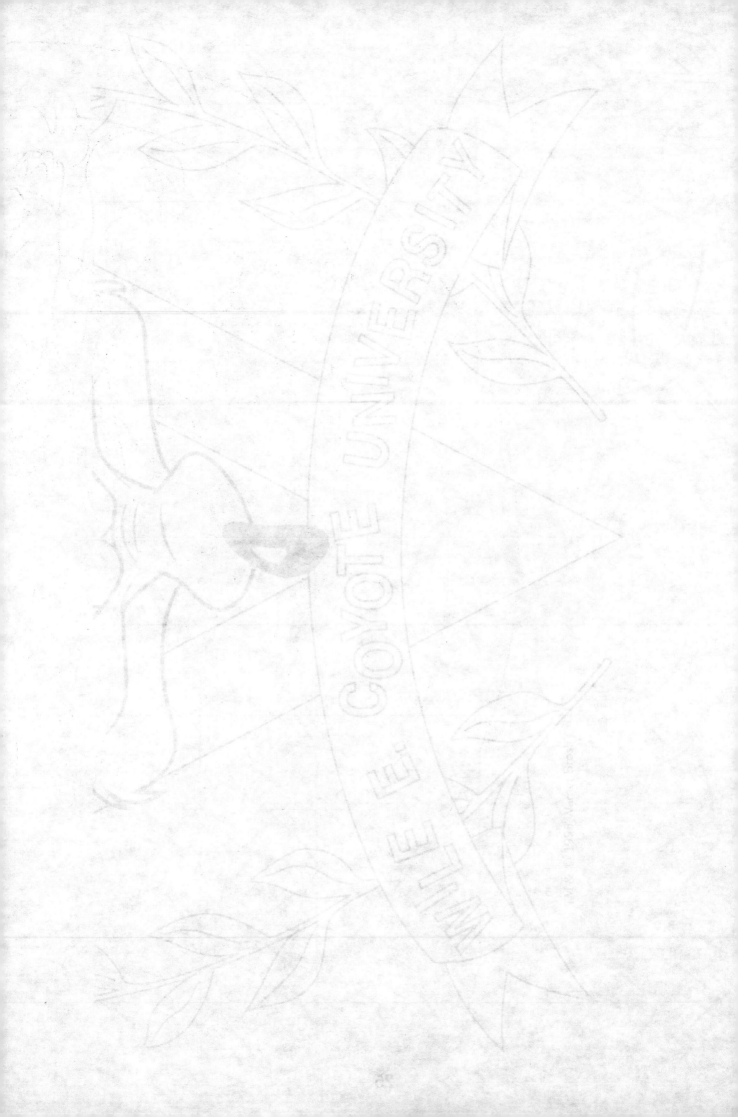

26

UNIVERSITY OF TASMANIA

27

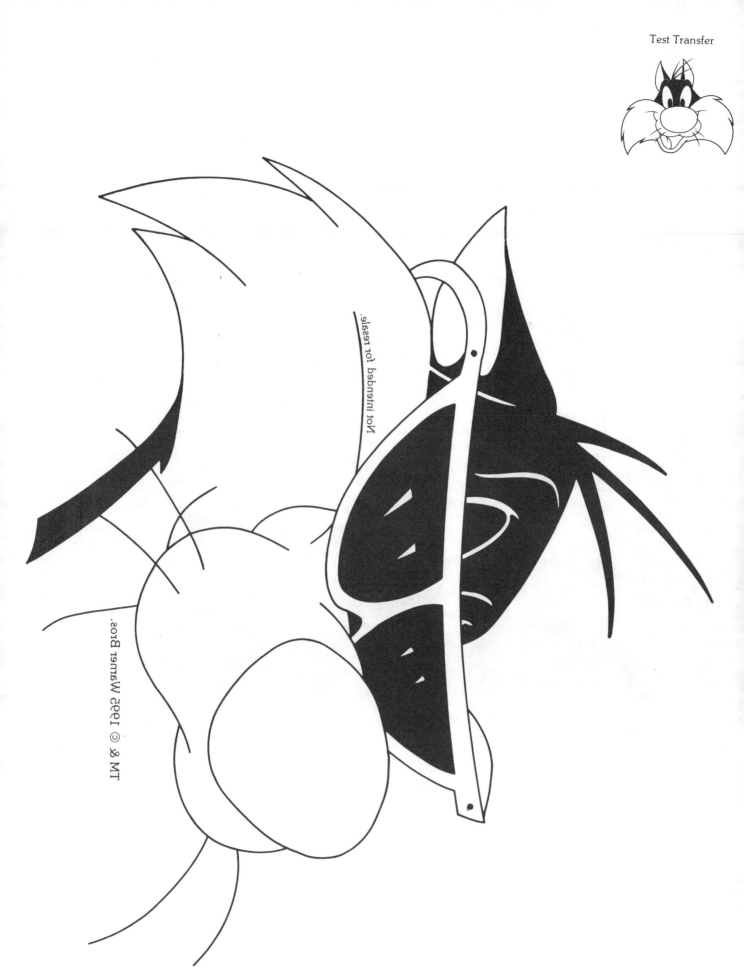

Not intended for resale.

TM & © 1995 Warner Bros.

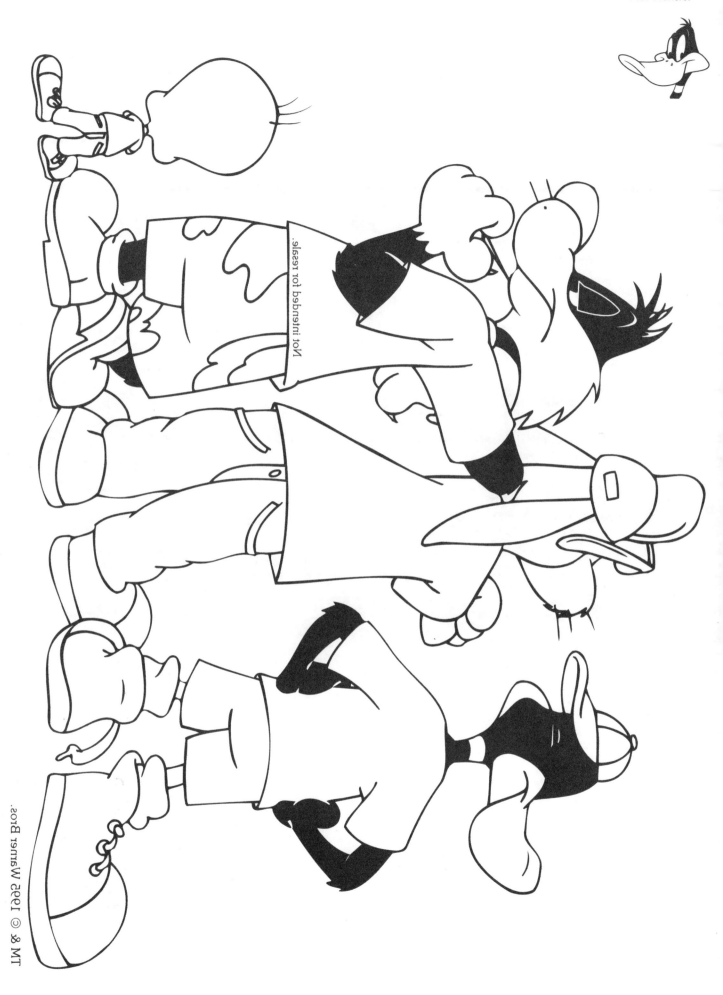

Not intended for resale.

36

40

Not intended for resale.

41

Not intended for resale.

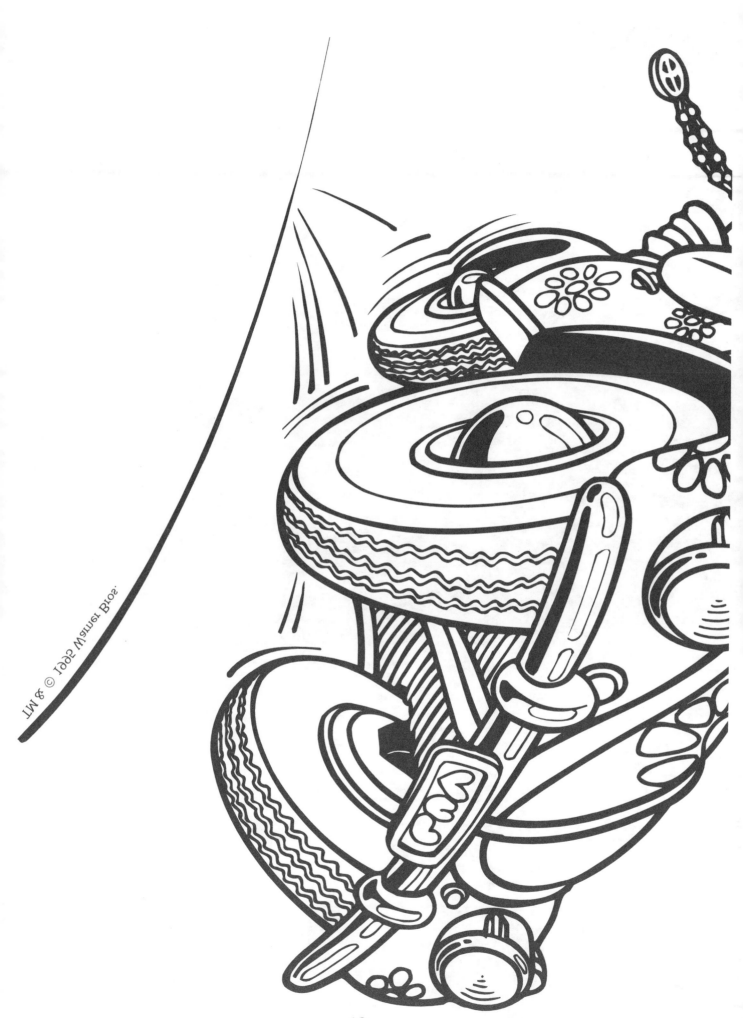

43

Not intended for resale

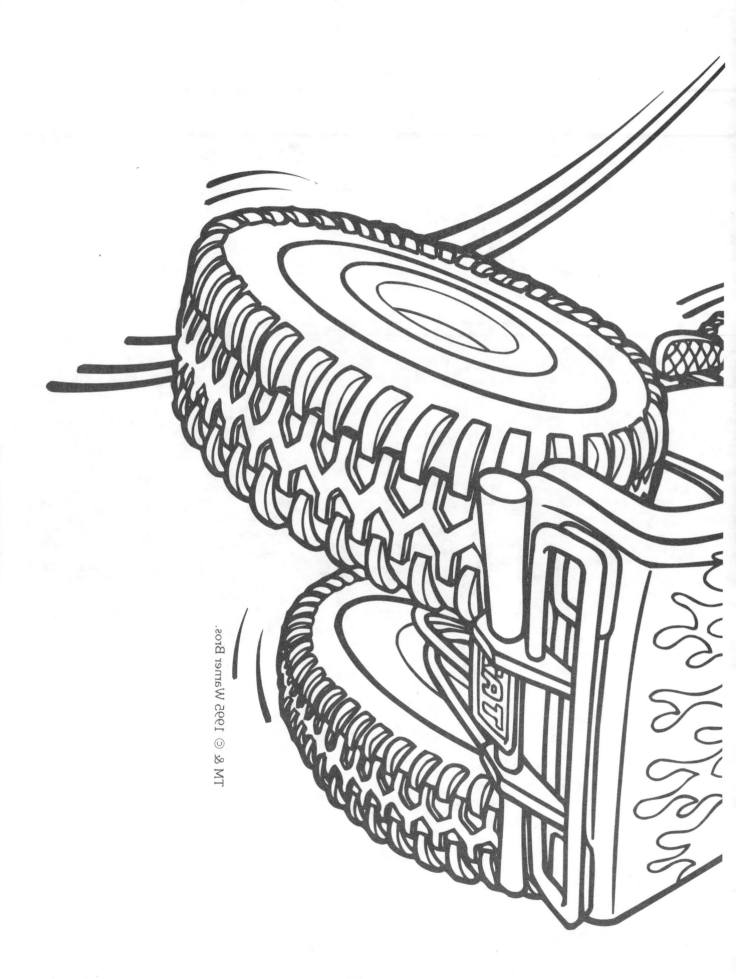

45

46

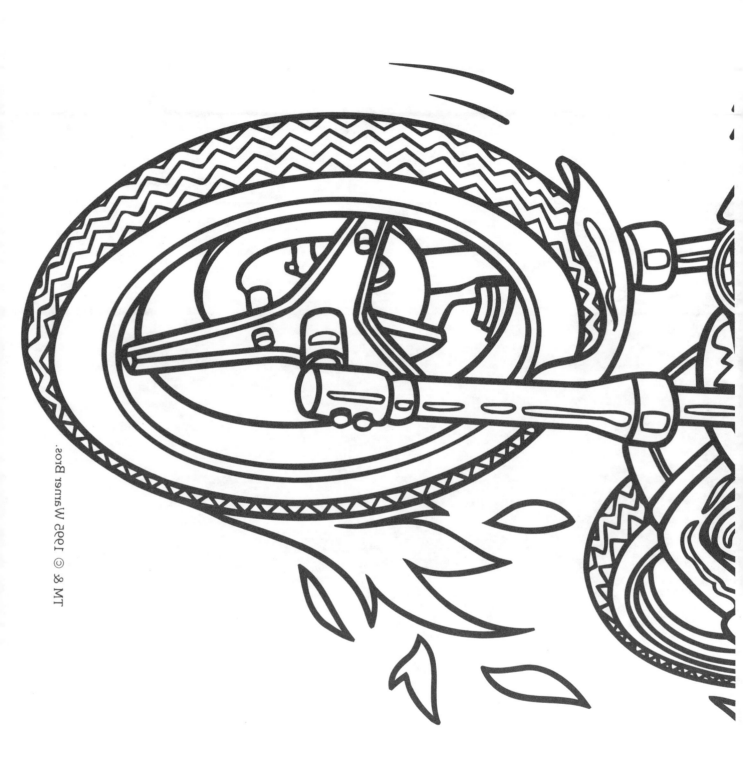

50

Not intended for resale.

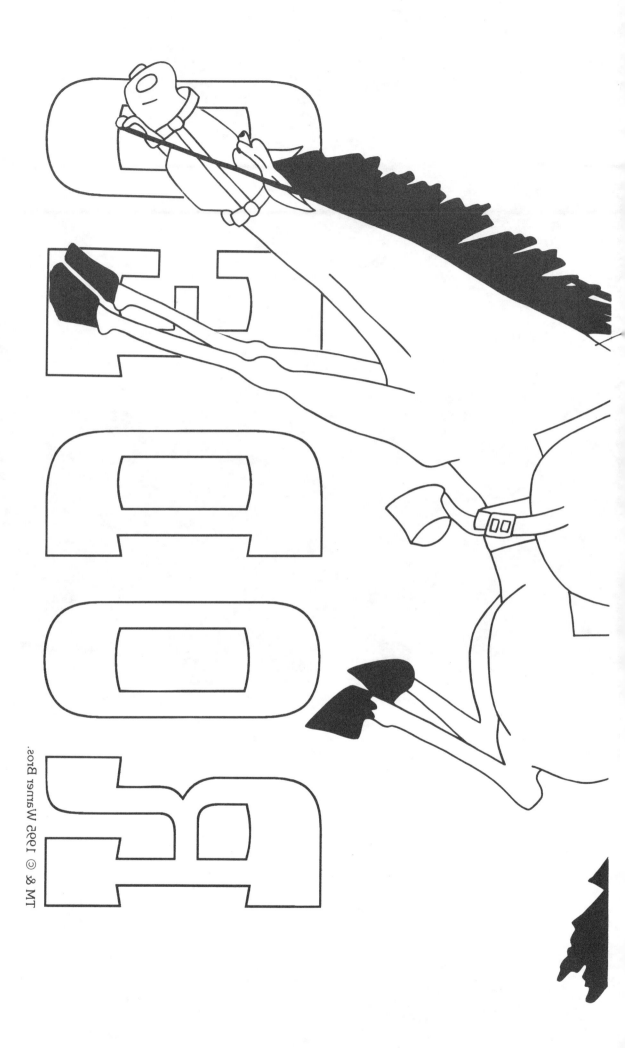

BODY

Test Transfer

Not intended for resale.

TM & © 1995 Warner Bros.

54

Not intended for resale.

Not intended for resale.

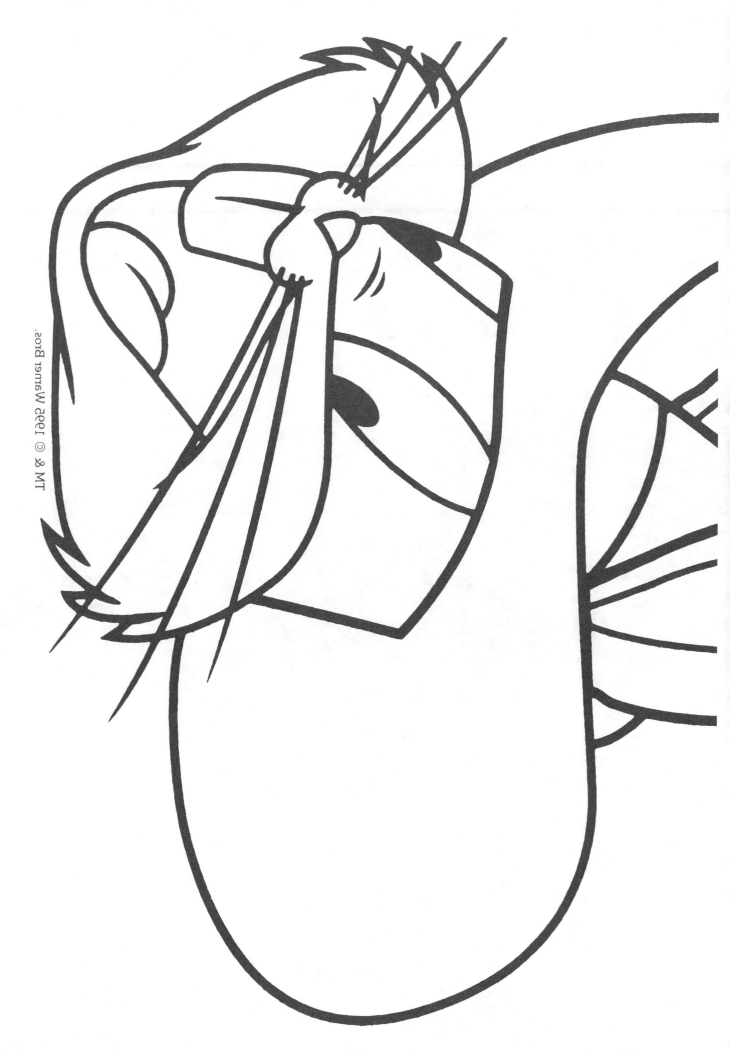

57

Not intended for resale.

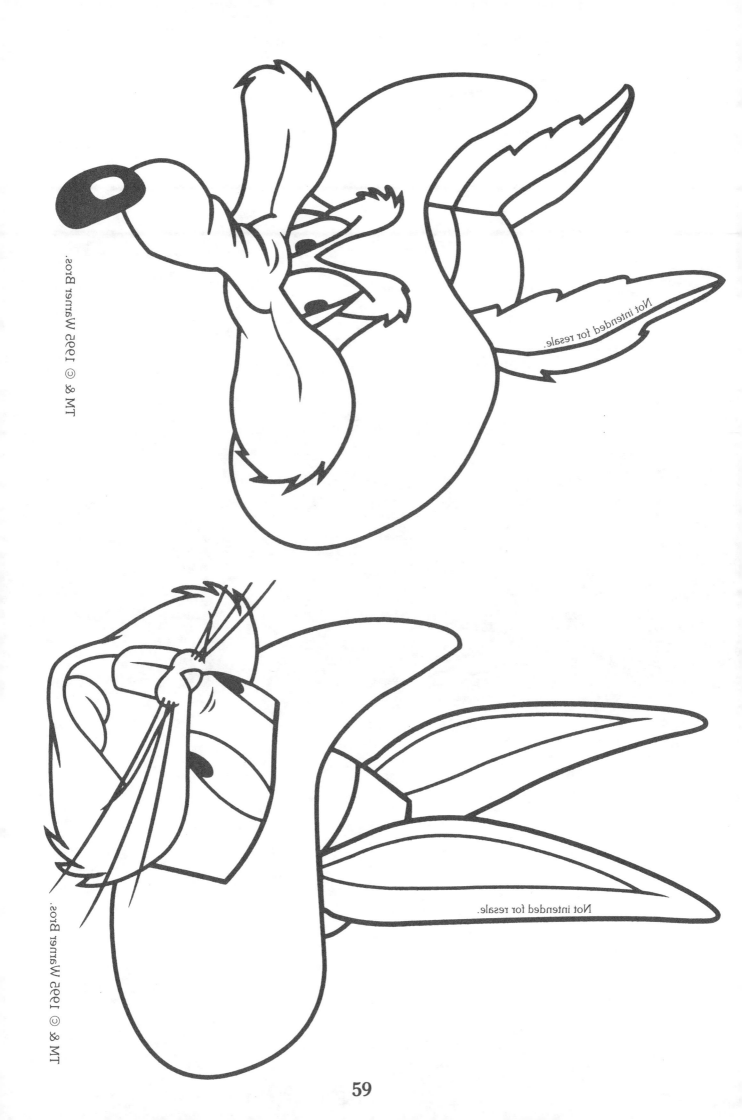

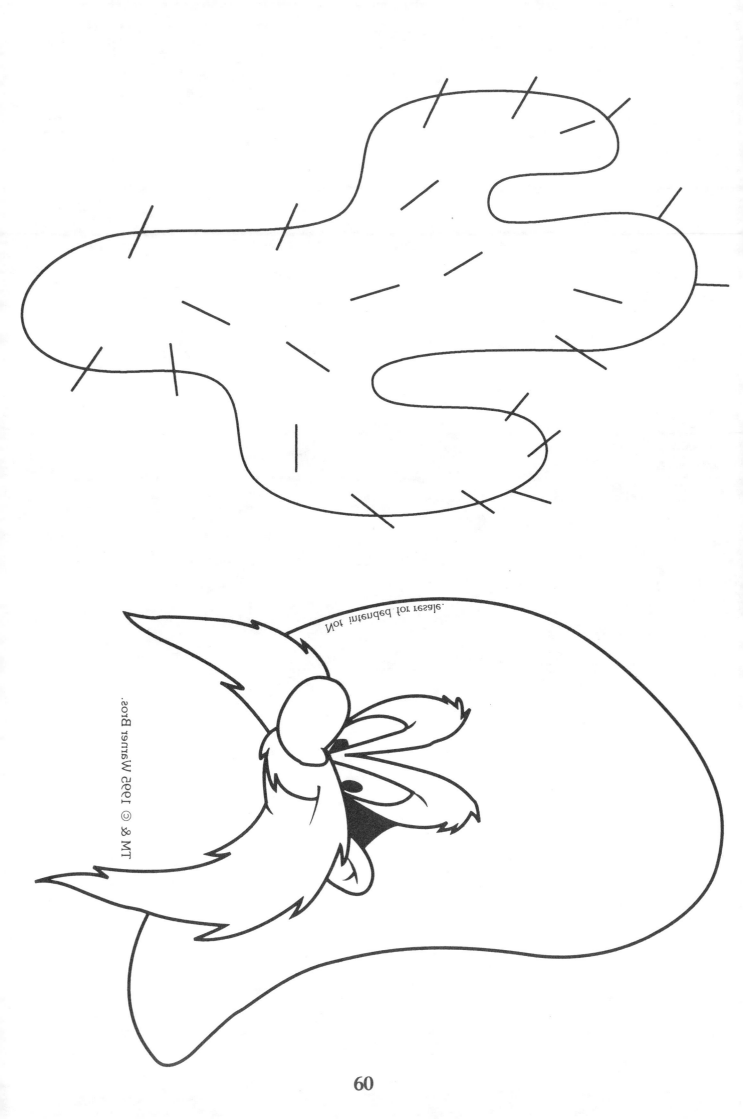

Not intended for resale.

TM & © 1995 Warner Bros.

60

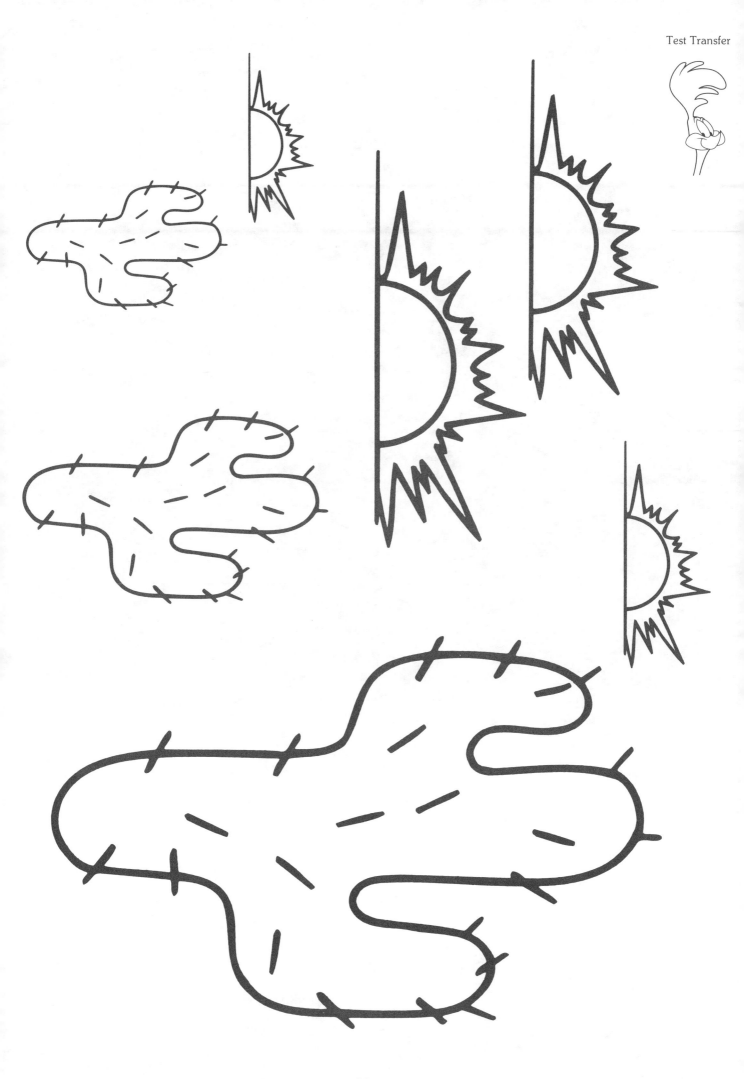

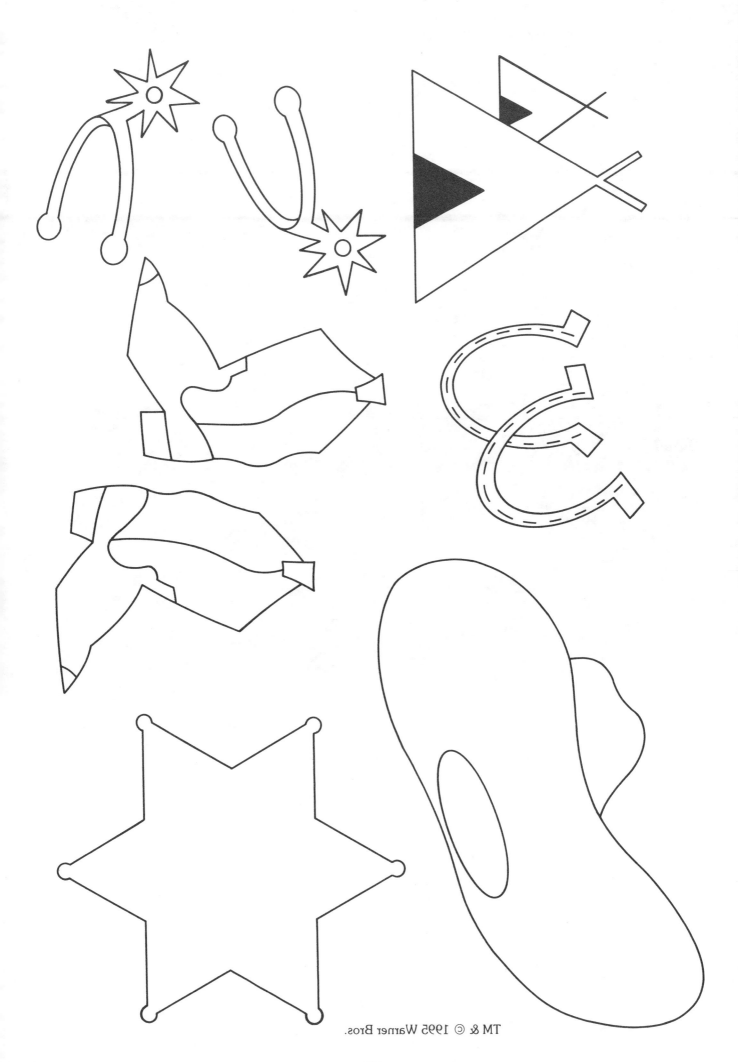

62

BE MINE
B-B-B-BE

Not intended for resale.

TM & © 1995 Warner Bros.

63

TONE DEVIL

Not intended for resale.

TM & © 1995 Warner Bros.

TWICK or TWEET

Not intended for resale.

TM & © 1995 Warner Bros.

Not intended for resale.

Not intended for resale.

72

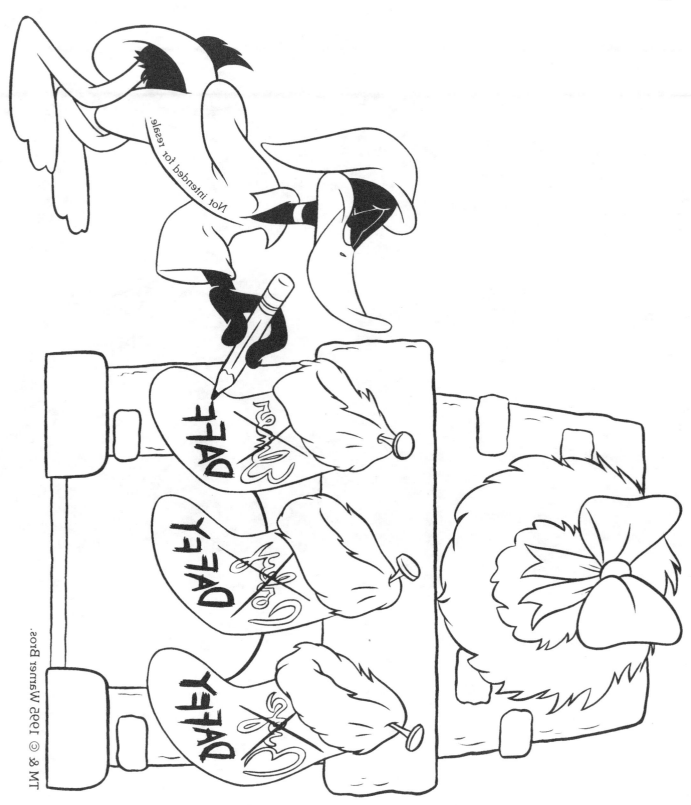

Not intended for resale.

Not intended for resale.

TM & © 1995 Warner Bros.

77

78

the picture

match

79

Not intended for resale.

81

Not intended for resale.

Not intended for resale.

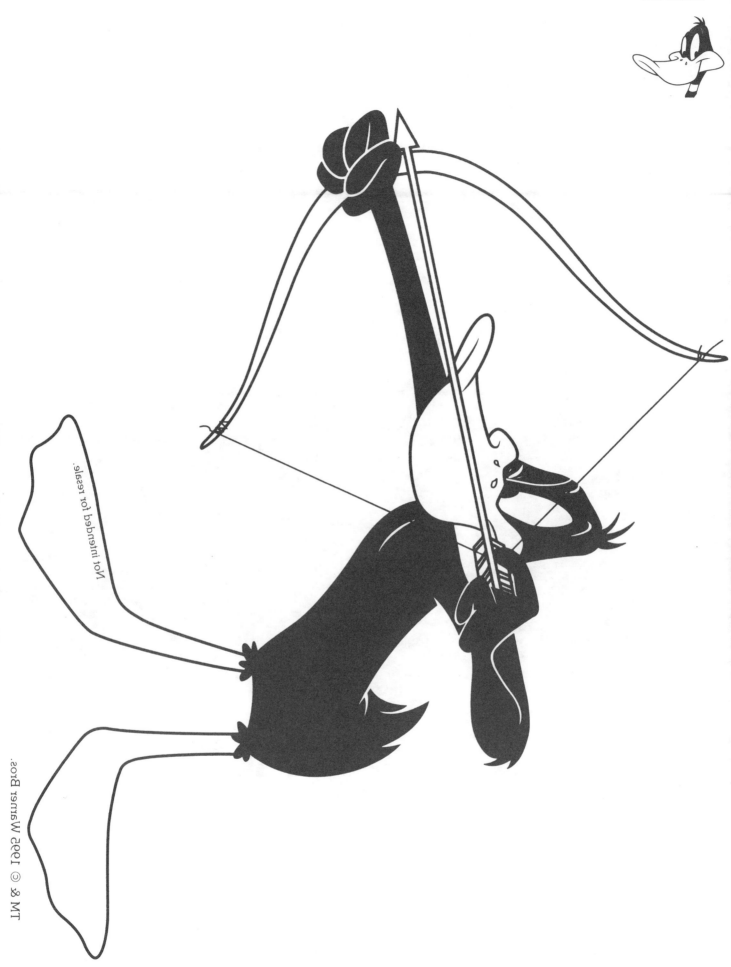

Not intended for resale.

Not intended for resale.

Not intended for resale.

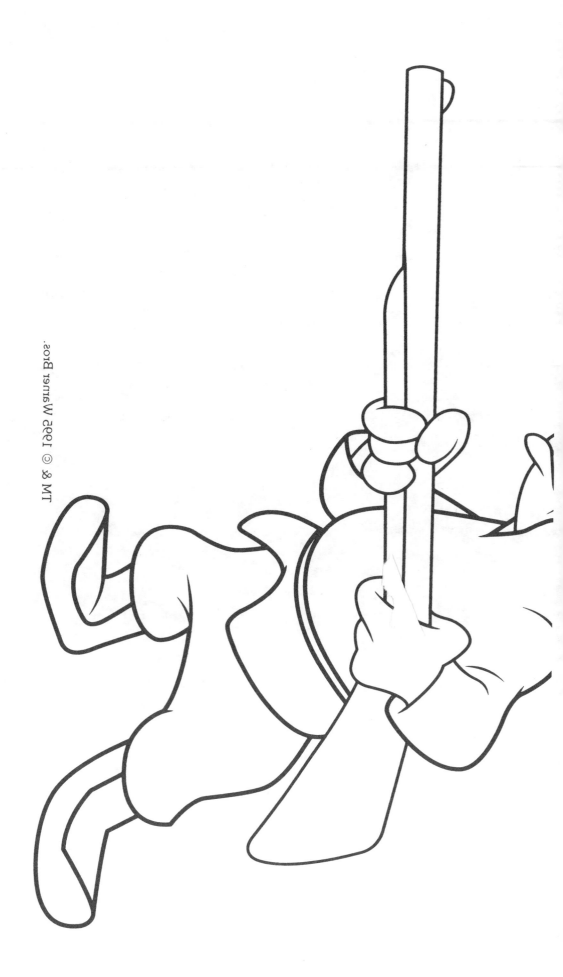

92

Not intended for resale.

Not intended for resale.

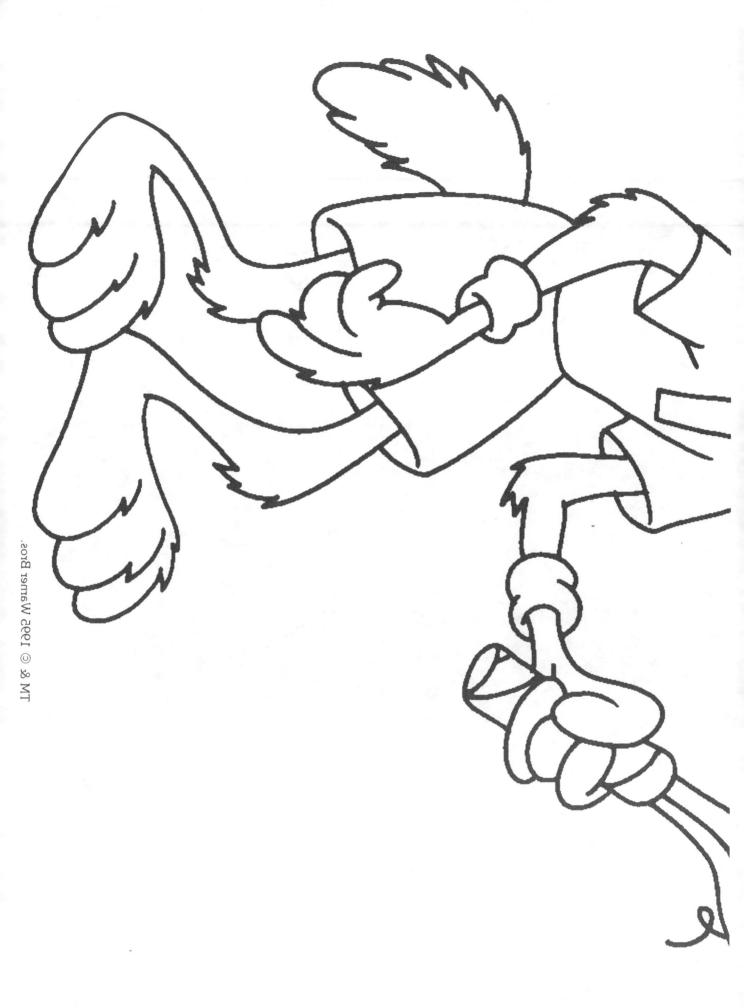

Not intended for resale.

TM & © 1995 Warner Bros.

Not intended for resale.

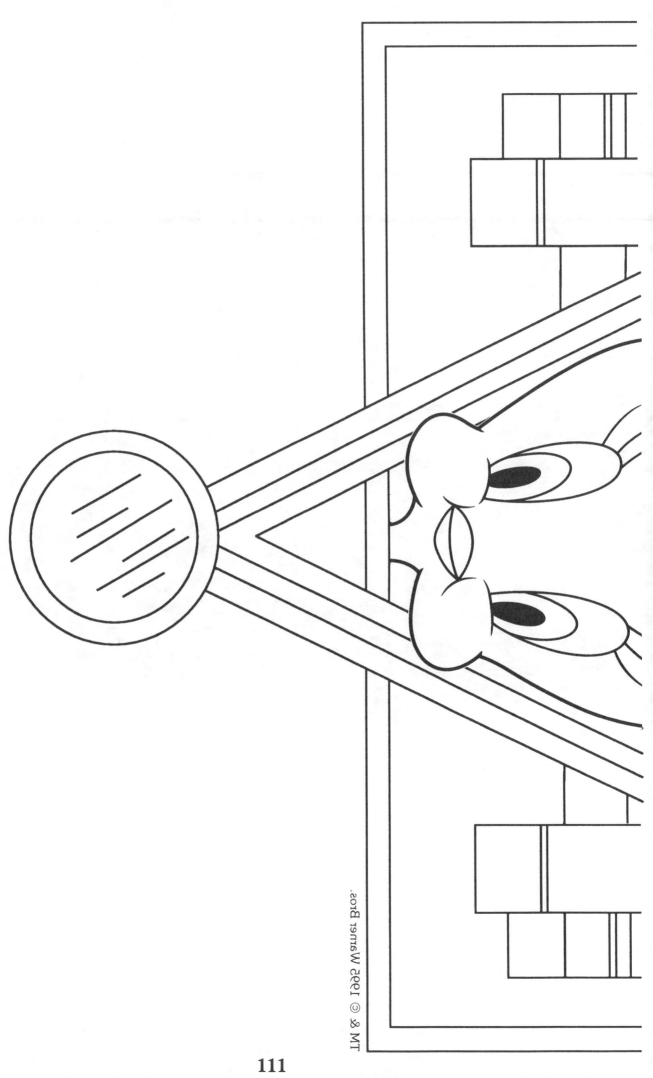

111

CLUB

TM & © 1995 Warner Bros.

115

PORKY PIG'S SWIMMING

CLUB

PLANET MARS

TWIN WINGS

Not intended for resale.

Not intended for resale.

123

$$A + B + C + \ldots$$

$$A + B + \sqrt{32}$$

$$(RR + -7)$$

DINNER

DINNER =

Not intended for resale.

Not intended for resale.

126

Not intended for resale.

Not intended for resale.

TM & © 1995 Warner Bros.

Not intended for resale.

BE
VE-WY
VE-WY
QUIET!

Not intended for resale.

137

Not intended for resale.

139

Not intended for resale.

TM & © 1995 Warner Bros.

Not intended for resale.

Not intended for resale.

143

WHERE'S MY GWANNY?

144

WHERE'S
MY
GWANNY?

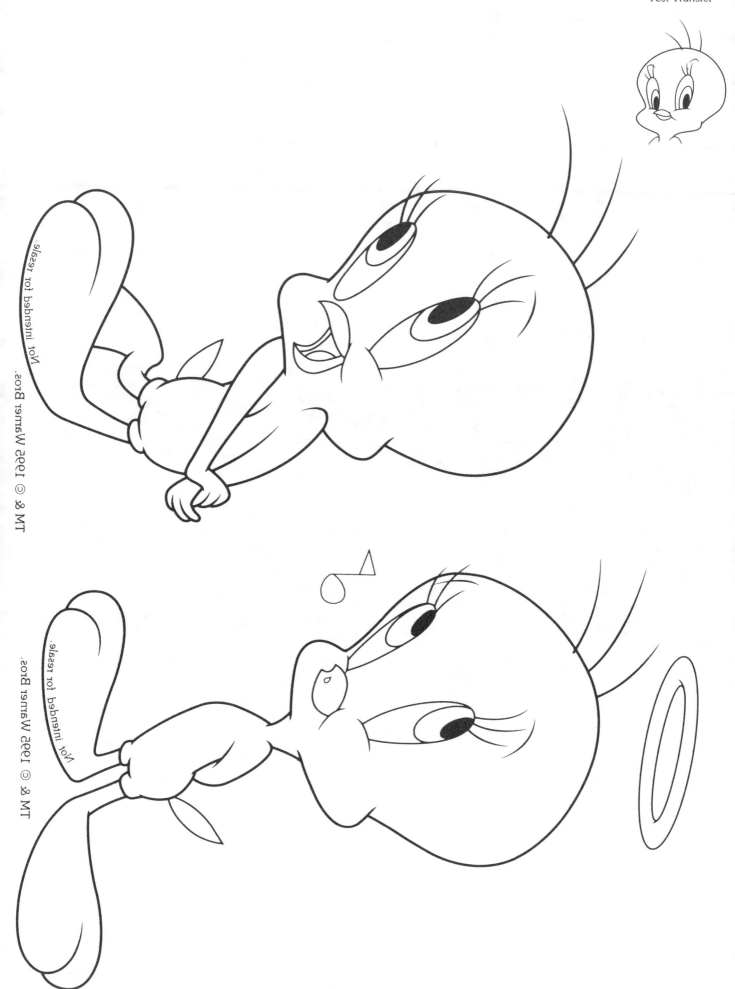

147

149

CARNIVAROUS
VULGARIS

Not intended for resale.

TM & © 1995 Warner Bros.

150

CARNIVAROUS

VULGARIS

Test Transfer

Not intended for resale.

TM & © 1995 Warner Bros.

151

Not intended for resale.

What's one tiny planet?

153

GO HOME
EaRThLiNgS

156

157

158

Not intended for resale.

160

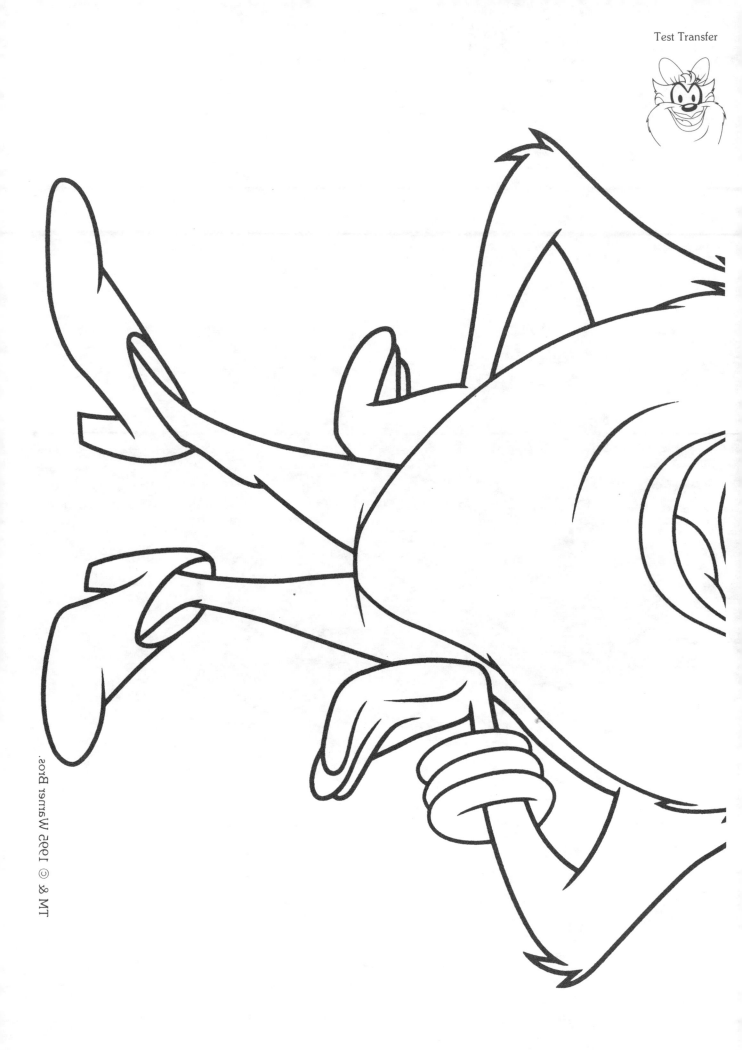

Not intended for resale.

TM & © 1995 Warner Bros.

Pepé Le Pew

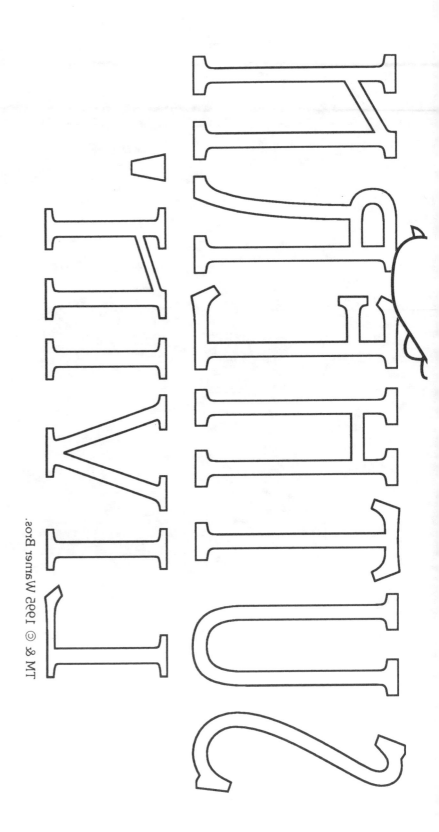

NIGHTMARE THEATER

Not intended for resale.

EUREKA!

170

SMOKING SECTION

SMOKING SECTION

Not intended for resale.

Not intended for resale.

ABCDEFG
HIJKLMN
OPQRSTU
VWXYZ
12345
67890

ABCDEFG
HIJKLMN
OPQRSTU
VWXYZ
12345
67890